3 1994 01357 3081

8|67

SAN  P9-DUU-656 RARY

AR PTS: 0.5

CELEBRATE HOLIDAYS

Celebrate Chinese New Year

Elaine A. Kule

J CHINESE NEW YEAR
394.261 KUL
Kule, Elaine A.
Celebrate Chinese New Year

$31.93
CENTRAL   31994013573081

A paper dragon is being used for a dragon dance.

Enslow Publishers, Inc.
40 Industrial Road
Box 398
Berkeley Heights, NJ 07922
USA

http://www.enslow.com

Copyright © 2006 by Enslow Publishers, Inc.

All rights reserved.

No part of this book may be reproduced by any means without the written permission of the publisher.

Library of Congress Cataloging-in-Publication Data

Kule, Elaine A.
  Celebrate Chinese New Year / Elaine A. Kule.
    p. cm. — (Celebrate holidays)
  Includes bibliographical references and index.
  ISBN 0-7660-2577-2
    1. Chinese New Year—Juvenile literature. I. Title. II. Series.
  GT4905.K85 2006
  394.261—dc22

                                          2005028106

Printed in the United States of America

10 9 8 7 6 5 4 3 2 1

To Our Readers: We have done our best to make sure all Internet Addresses in this book were active and appropriate when we went to press. However, the author and the publisher have no control over and assume no liability for the material available on those Internet sites or on other Web sites they may link to. Any comments or suggestions can be sent by e-mail to comments@enslow.com or to the address on the back cover.

Every effort has been made to locate all copyright holders of material used in this book. If any errors or omissions have occurred, corrections will be made in future editions of this book.

Illustration Credits: © 1999 Artville, LLC., p. 8; Associated Press, pp. 52, 65, 68, 76, 80, 84, 87, 92, 95; Corel Corporation, pp. 1, 4, 7, 33, 43, 45, 47, 55, 59, 61; Enslow Publishers, Inc., p. 62; Courtesy of Government Printing Office, Republic of China, p. 38; © 2005 JupiterImages, pp. 5, 6 (both), 9, 13, 20 (all), 21 (all), 22 (all), 23 (all), 24 (all), 25, 30, 31, 35, 40, 50, 53, 70, 71, 74, 81; © Panorama Images/The Image Works, p. 37; Taiwan Government Information Office, p. 42; craft and photos by Beth Townsend, pp. 98, 99.

Cover Illustration: Corel Corporation.

CONTENTS

The people made loud noises to keep the beast Nian away.

A Beast Called Nian

The Chinese New Year holiday began centuries ago. Over time, it acquired customs that spanned generations. The following story explains how some of these traditions started. It takes place in ancient China and features a beast called Nian.

Nian slept all year until the thirtieth day of the last month in the Chinese calendar. On that day, the creature traveled from place to place, beating or killing people and animals.

One New Year's Eve, Nian arrived at a village where several boys were having a whip-cracking contest to see who could make the most noise. The loud sounds terrified the monster so much that it ran to another village. There it saw some bright red clothing hanging on a line to dry. Nian was scared of that, too.

Fleeing to a third village, Nian stopped at a house and looked through a crack in the door. A lit candle made the monster feel so dizzy that it panicked and left the village.

People soon realized that Nian was afraid of loud noises, the color red, and light. During every Chinese New Year season, they exploded firecrackers, wore red clothes, and lit candles and fireworks, especially on New Year's Eve.

Fireworks were lit to keep the beast away.

Their plan worked. The beast was too frightened to ever bother them again.[1]

The Chinese New Year had its beginnings before people even knew what a year was. It started with a great need for an everyday necessity—the calendar.

Long Ago and Far Away

China is the oldest living civilization, dating back to before written history began. Scientists believe that prehistoric human beings may have lived in parts of China about 2 million years ago.[1]

Tracing the Chinese New Year's earliest beginnings requires studying the development of the calendar—a system of measuring and recording the passage of time. Because the Chinese people felt an important connection between man and nature, their astronomers—scientists who study the sun, the moon, and the stars—believed that life on Earth depended on knowing as much as possible about the sky above them.

The Early Chinese Calendars

By around 2700 B.C., astronomers had a more practical reason for studying astronomy.

Most of ancient China's population were farmers who did not always know the best time to plant crops. A small or ruined harvest was often the result. People needed to know when to avoid rainy or snowy seasons, and when the weather would be hot and the soil dry.

Chinese emperors, or rulers, oversaw all astronomical work. People believed that emperors were blessed by the gods, and rulers wanted their subjects to remain faithful to them. If an emperor could not solve the farmers' problems, it could mean the gods were displeased with him, and people might become disloyal.

Emperors were also worried that information might be used by people hoping to seize control of their empire. Studies were done secretly, and anyone who was not part of the emperor's court was forbidden to study astronomy.[2]

A legendary figure, Huang Di, also known as the Yellow Emperor, is believed to have created the first Chinese calendar in approximately 2637 B.C. After watching the moon's changing appearance, or phases, he and his scientists developed a lunar calendar.

Historians believe that Huang Di's chief astronomer, Ta Nao, created "the system of cyclical characters." In this system, ten days equaled one week, and three such weeks equaled one month. Days were counted by pairing symbols called the Ten Heavenly Stems with other symbols called the Twelve Earthly Branches, in sequential order. It took six repetitions of the set of Ten Stems and five repetitions of the Twelve Branches to complete the cycle, a total of sixty days. Cycles were used to name years during the first century.[3]

More Developments

The early calendar was a beginning, but farmers still needed to account for the sun's position in the sky to know when to plant crops. Chinese legends claim that in approximately 2254 B.C., Emperor Yao, a descendant of Huang Di, ordered his astrologers to learn more about the cycle of changing seasons.

Important developments were made during the era known as Imperial China, when dynasties—a series of successive rulers from the same family or group—led the country.

Astronomers of the Shang dynasty (seventeenth–eleventh century B.C.) made a lunar calendar based on months, the time between one new moon to the next. Each month was between twenty-nine and thirty days long.[4]

Heng-O and the Twelve Chinese Moons

Several myths and legends were created in ancient China to help explain the mysteries of the universe. In "Heng-O and the Twelve Chinese Moons," people thought there were twelve moons just as there were twelve months in one year. They also thought there were ten suns, just as there were ten days in the Chinese week. The mother of the twelve moons was also the mother of the ten suns.

At the beginning of each month, the mother, Heng-O, washed her children in a lake at the far western side of the world. Then each moon, one after the other, traveled in a chariot for a monthlong journey to reach the opposite, east side of the world.

There, the suns started their journey. It was believed that the moons were made of water, and either a rabbit or a toad lived in them.[5]

Measuring Time: Sundials and Water Clocks

The ancient Chinese people measured the passing of days by using astronomical instruments called sundials and water clocks. A sundial shows the time of day by the position of the sha- dow of a gnomon, the raised part of a sundial. Because the angle of sunlight changes as the earth travels around the sun, measuring time from sunlight will not always be accurate.

A water clock is a hollow instrument that lets water drop at a steady rate from a small hole near the bottom. Marks inside the instrument mea-

This is a working Chinese water clock.

sure how much time has passed as the water level reaches each mark. Since the flow of water is diffi- cult to control, these clocks were not a dependable way to tell time.[6]

The Seasons: Solstices and Equinoxes

In the Northern Hemisphere—the half of the earth between the North Pole and the equator—the winter solstice signals the first day of winter. It falls on December 21 or 22. At this time, the earth's axis is tipped away from the sun. The Northern Hemisphere receives less sunlight and the days are shorter.

On about June 21, the summer solstice marks the beginning of summer. At this time, the sun is at its most northern position and the days are longer.

On about September 21 and March 20, the sun is directly above the earth's equator. Day and night are of equal length all over the world. In the Northern Hemisphere, the March equinox, which is also called the vernal equinox, marks the beginning of spring. The September equinox signals the beginning of autumn and is called the autumnal equinox.

In the Southern Hemisphere—the half of the earth between the South Pole and the equator—summer and winter are reversed. For example, it is summer in Australia (the Southern Hemisphere) when it is winter in the U.S. (the Northern Hemisphere).[7]

The Story of Wan-nian-li or the Perpetual Calendar

A familiar legend about the early Chinese calendar takes place during the Shang dynasty. The story is about a young man named Wan-nian, who is said to have invented the perpetual calendar, called wan-nian-li, which shows the day of the week a date will fall in any year.

Working on his own, Wan-nian calculated time by measuring the length of shadows during the year with a gnomon—the raised part of a sundial—and the length of each day using a water clock.

By noting the longest and shortest days of the year, Wan-nian learned about the two solstices and two equinoxes. He also discovered how many days there were in a year. Eventually Wan-nian made a simple yet fairly accurate calendar. He had to keep the work secret, however, because only King Zuyi's astronomers were allowed to study the sky.

Since everything about the calendar and astronomy fell under King Zuyi's control, he oversaw the ongoing work. Like everyone else, especially the farmers whose crops were sometimes planted at the wrong time, he was unhappy with the current calendar.

The man in charge of fixing the calendar was an incapable official named A Heng. When King Zuyi confronted him about measuring the seasons incorrectly, A Heng said it was the farmers' fault for somehow angering the gods, and bad crops were their punishment. He said the farmers should offer a sacrifice, perhaps an animal or an object, so that the seasons would happen at the right time.

The king believed him. He gave orders for a large tower to be built as a tribute to the gods. When Wan-nian heard of these plans, he knew that such costly and time-consuming work would be useless. He felt he should warn the ruler, and after some pleading with the king's guards, he had a meeting with him.

Wan-nian showed King Zuyi his charts and findings. He explained A Heng's errors in calculating the seasons, and that poor crops were not the work of angry gods.

The king liked what he heard. He hired Wan-nian to learn more about astronomy and gave him a group of assistants.

When A Heng learned about Wan-nian and the new assignment, he was worried about losing his job. He decided to hire someone to kill Wan-nian.

Wan-nian worked long hours in a place that was always guarded, so murdering him would not be easy. Three years passed. Growing impatient, the hired killer finally chose a bow and arrow to complete his mission. Just as Wan-nian stopped by an opened window, the killer took aim and struck him in the arm. Wan-nian's assistants shouted for help, and the shooter was quickly found. He and A Heng were later questioned and executed.

Sometime later, the king visited Wan-nian to see how he was feeling. Wan-nian showed him his most recent efforts and then mentioned that it was midnight and the start of the new year. King Zuyi said that since spring marks the beginning of a new year, the time should be called the Spring Festival. Grateful for Wan-nian's loyalty and hard work, the ruler invited him to his palace so they could welcome the new year together.

Wan-nian was promoted to Minister of the Astronomical Bureau. He stayed at the job, improving and correcting the calendar, until he was old. When he finished his work, he gave it to the pleased ruler. The *Wan-nian-li*, or perpetual calendar, was eventually distributed throughout the king's empire.[8]

The story has remained an important part of Chinese folklore and culture. To this day, many people decorate their homes with a small statue or picture of an old man with a long white beard. It is Wan-nian, who became the God of Longevity, or long life.

Ancient farmers used the word *nian* to mean the amount of time required to grow one crop of grain. Since it took one year, *nian* became the word for the start of one crop cycle to another, or one year.[9]

The Solar Calendar

By about 444 B.C., scientists calculated that a solar year had 365¼ days.[10] About two centuries later, Chinese astronomers created a solar calendar that let farmers know when to plant crops. It divided the year into twenty-four sections, with each section about fifteen days apart. The names of each section are listed below.[11]

Beginning of Spring	Beginning of Autumn
Rain Water	**End of Heat**
Waking of Insects	**White Dew**
Spring Equinox	**Autumn Equinox**
Pure Brightness	**Cold Dew**
Corn Rain	**Descent of Frost**

Beginning of Summer	Beginning of Winter
Grain Full	Slight Snow
Grain in the Ear	Great Snow
Summer Solstice	Winter Solstice
Slight Heat	Slight Cold
Great Heat	Great Cold

The Tournament of the Twelve Animals

By approximately 600 B.C., Chinese astronomers were using the cyclical system of pairing Ten Heavenly Stems with Twelve Earthly Branches to count years, as well as days. The scientists also paired each cycle of twelve animal years with the five elements they believed made up the universe—wood, fire, earth, metal, and water—creating a sixty-year cycle.[12]

The astronomers thought using animals for symbols would help people identify and remember the Twelve Earthly Branches more easily. The following legend tells how and in what order these creatures were selected.

When the Jade Emperor, "ruler of the heavens," announced he would pick animals to symbolize the twelve years, all the animals rushed to his palace, hoping to be chosen.

Not knowing which animals to pick, or which month each should represent, the emperor decided to hold a tournament, or contest, the next morning. The tournament would be based on the animals' skills and character traits. There would be twelve categories and twelve gold plaques awarded for each ranking in the contest. The Elephant was chosen as judge because he was honest and fair.

When the Cat learned of the tournament, he asked Rat to wake him the following morning and go with him to the event. The Rat agreed, but he thought the Cat might beat him in the contest. Instead of keeping his word, he crept to the tournament area alone, while it was still dark.

The Ox was already there and the contest started quickly. Rat climbed into Ox's ear and bit as hard as he could. After the Ox begged Rat to stop, the Elephant declared Rat the first-place winner of a gold plaque.

The Ox said he should receive the second-place prize. Just then the Horse appeared, demanding that he get a chance to compete. The Elephant gave them a challenge: try to pull a loaded wagon the farthest.

The Horse struggled until he had to quit. The Ox was given the second gold plaque, while the Horse ran off, upset about his loss.

Just then the Cat ran up on the tournament stage, angry because Rat did not wake him. The Elephant said, "You unwisely trusted someone who was sneaky. You may, however, compete for a lower category."

The Cat glared at Rat, knowing they would always be enemies, and they have.

The Tiger appeared, challenging Cat to a battle for the next prize. When the Tiger leaped toward him, the Cat scrambled up the nearest tree. The Tiger was too heavy to climb after him. Because he ran away, the Cat lost his place as a contestant and was omitted from the group of zodiac animals.

Suddenly, the skies grew dark and

stormy. A Dragon fell from the heavens, landing on the tournament platform. He yelled at the Tiger, "Leave, or I will bring thunder and lightning down on you."

The Tiger was unafraid. He challenged him to a race, won it easily, and received the next gold plaque. The Elephant gave the Dragon an award for competing well. The creature was about to accept his prize when a Rabbit hopped on stage and grabbed it.

The Rabbit said to the Dragon, "Please do not be angry. I know you are powerful. But my long ears give me sharp hearing. I can tell the direction of the wind and rain and can warn people to take cover. Because of my skill, your place should be after me."

The Rabbit's words made sense to the Dragon, and he agreed to take the lower prize. Before he could, a Snake slithered on stage. She said she deserved the award because of her beauty.

"Mistress Snake," said the Dragon, "this is a tournament of skills and ability. It is not a beauty contest."

The audience laughed at the Snake, who grew embarrassed. Dragon felt badly, and since they were of similar species, he suggested she receive the next plaque. No one objected, and the Snake was pleased.

The Horse returned, annoyed that only a few gold plaques remained. He complained to the judge, who said, "By leaving the tournament, you lost your right to an award. Still, as a fair judge, I will award you the seventh-place prize because of your talent." The Horse accepted the gold plaque.

A Monkey climbed up on stage and said, "I bet no one would dare compete with me!"

A Sheep leaped onto the tournament platform and said, "Stop bragging! I am sure you are not up to my standards!"

The Monkey said, "I can climb mountains and trees. What can you do?"

The Sheep said, "I cannot climb trees, but I help Man by giving meat, milk, wool, and sheepskin. What do you do for People?"

The audience applauded, and the Monkey admitted defeat. The Sheep took the eighth-place award and the Monkey accepted the ninth-place prize.

Suddenly a large Dog jumped on the stage and demanded one of the three remaining plaques. Then a Rooster flew on the podium and started crowing skillfully. The Dog bared his teeth angrily. He was about to attack the bird, but the Rooster flew up and started pecking at him until he yelped in pain. Still, the Dog would not give in.

The judge ordered the Dog to back down. The tenth prize was given to the Rooster and the Dog received the eleventh award.

Only one plaque was left, but no one wanted it. Finally a slow-moving Pig moved onto the stage. The audience called out insults but the Pig ignored them.

The Elephant said, "The Pig is not angered by your comments. He deserves credit for that, so I will give him the final prize." With that, the Pig became the twelfth zodiac animal.[13]

◆ ◆ ◆ ◆

The story is one of several legends explaining the selection and order of the twelve zodiac animals. At first, the creatures had no particular symbolism or meaning, but over time, people gave them character traits. They used these traits to help predict the personality and fortune of people born during each year. Turn to pages 77–78 for a complete list of these animals and their traits.[14]

Yin and Yang

The ancient Chinese noticed that many of nature's daily events repeated themselves in cycles, such as the rising and setting of the sun and the phases of the moon. Astronomers called these balancing forces yin and yang. They believed that when the opposites of cold, dark, negative, and feminine (yin) connected with heat, light, positive, and masculine (yang), the combination influences the future of all creatures and things.

Scientists thought the forces of yin and yang kept order in the universe, an idea that led Chinese astronomers to create a lunar-solar calendar showing the sun's and moon's activities.[15]

Modern Times

For centuries, dynasties kept changing the Chinese calendar, and the first day of a new year kept changing, too. Nearly a hundred different Chinese calendars were created.

From about 140 B.C. to the present time, however, the Chinese New Year has been celebrated on the first day of the first lunar month of the Chinese calendar.[16]

In 1912, when the Republic of China was founded, the commonly used Gregorian calendar was introduced to the nation. Although people still celebrated the Chinese New Year, it was not considered an official holiday.

In 1927, the National Congress of China declared the Spring Festival, or *Ch'un-chieh*, as the Chinese New Year. In 1949, at the First Congress of the People's Republic of China, January 1 was called *Yüan-tan* and made a holiday. The Chinese New Year was made a holiday too, with three official days given for its celebration.[17]

Facts About the Chinese Calendar

◆ The Chinese calendar is solar and lunar. It is based on the positions of the sun and the moon.

◆ The new moon is the first day of a lunar month.

◆ The Chinese New Year, also called the Chinese Lunar New Year, falls between January 21 and February 20, the second new moon after the winter solstice.

◆ A year is divided into twelve months, each having twenty-nine or thirty days.

◆ A lunar year has twelve months containing 354 days. The solar year has 365¼ days. To keep the two even, a leap month, or extra month, is added to the calendar about every three years.

◆ Every nineteen years, eleven leap months are added to keep the lunar calendar from falling behind the solar calendar.[18]

Calendars From Other Cultures

The Hebrew calendar, also called a Jewish calendar, began in approximately 1050 B.C. It is still used today for holiday and religious purposes, such as determining on which days religious holidays will fall.

The modern Jewish calendar uses a lunar and solar system, with months based on the moon's

What Is the Gregorian Calendar?

The Gregorian calendar is the system used by countries throughout the world. Each year has 365 days, or 366 days in the case of a leap year. The extra day becomes February 29.

The calendar was named for a Roman Catholic pope, Gregory XIII. In 1578, on the advice of astronomers, he officially corrected errors in the previous calendar. That calendar, the Julian, was named for Julius Caesar, a Roman emperor, and had been in use for fifteen hundred years.[19]

phases and years based on the sun's position in the sky. The calendar has twelve months. Each month alternates between twenty-nine and thirty days. Religious holidays start at sunset, officially considered the start of a new day.[20]

The Islamic day also begins at sunset. Muslims also use a seven-day week, although they number rather than name the days of the week. Friday, however, is an exception. Called the Day of Assembly, it is dedicated to prayer.

The Islamic calendar is based on a lunar cycle. It has twelve months, each of which has twenty-nine or thirty days.[21]

◆ ◆ ◆ ◆

Although many changes were made along the way, the Chinese calendar became the longest-running system of time measurement. After the Gregorian calendar was introduced in China in 1912, however, the Chinese calendar was used mostly for noting traditional festivals.

While the Chinese New Year falls on a different date each year, many of its ancient customs have stayed the same. The holiday, with its spirited and meaningful rituals, has influenced several art forms and enhanced the Chinese culture. Over the years, as people immigrated to other countries, they shared their heritage and enriched other civilizations as well.

An actor performs a traditional dance during Chinese New Year.

3

The Cultural Importance of the Chinese New Year

O ver time, the Chinese New Year advanced several forms of creative expression: storytelling, cooking, art, paper crafts, music, dance, drama, poetry, calligraphy, horticulture, and flower arranging. The holiday brought much to a country whose rich culture is admired throughout the world.

Storytelling

Long before there were books, the Chinese people created stories: for entertainment, to help explain what was difficult to understand, or to teach a moral lesson. A folktale often told among professional storytellers is "Shen-shu and Yu-lu, the Two Door Guardians."

The story is about two brothers, Shen-shu and Yu-lu. Tall, strong, and brave, they lived in small houses on a beautiful mountaintop in ancient China. Their job was to care for a peach tree orchard. Guarding the orchard were two tigers who the brothers had tamed just by looking at them.

The brothers worked hard and the peaches grew large and sweet. It was said that the fruit granted people longevity. The brothers gave them to anyone who was poor or ill.

A mean prince lived nearby. He wanted the orchard and led an army of soldiers to attack the brothers. It was a long battle, but Shen-shu, Yu-lu, and the tigers won. The prince went home angrier than ever.

One night, the brothers were awakened by noises. They went outside and saw creatures with green faces, sharp teeth, and huge red eyes. The group ran to them, but the men were not afraid.

The two brothers
lived on a
mountaintop
in China.

Shen-shu grabbed a large peachwood branch and whipped each attacker. Yu lu tied each fallen creature with a long rope.

The brothers let their hungry tigers gobble the terrible monsters, who were really the wicked prince and his men. Many people heard about the amazing story.

Years later, after the brothers died, their images were painted on peachwood tablets. These tablets were displayed during the Chinese New Year holiday to keep homes safe from evil spirits.[1]

Cooking

Few cultures have been more admired for their delicious cooking than the Chinese. Dishes are uniquely flavored and prepared, with many recipes handed down over several centuries. Some of these foods are served especially for the Chinese New Year holiday.

A Chinese New Year's Eve meal may start with the "Broth of Prosperity," a chicken soup with egg dumplings. Other dumplings, called *yuanbao* or *jiaozi*, may be boiled, pan-fried, and dipped in seasoning, such as soy sauce or vinegar. The dumplings are filled with chopped meat, fish, and cabbage. Some holiday dumplings may have one of

Many families prepare dumplings for their Chinese New Year feast.

eight symbolic items inside, such as peanuts for a long life, candy for a sweet year, coins for wealth, and walnuts for peace.

A dessert prepared especially for the New Year is *niangao*, which means "the cake of the year." It is a sweet and sticky rice cake made mostly from a gooey rice flour. A smooth texture to the cake means a good year for the family.

Preparing *niangao* begins with rice flour that is steamed for hours until it turns solid. A plain *niangao* has only sugar, oil, and sesame seeds added. Other types may include yams, red dates, or peanuts.[2]

In Chinese cooking, foods are usually boiled or steamed. They may also be stir-fried quickly in oil and cooked in a wok—a big, round, metal pan with handles.[3]

Art and Paper Crafts

Painting, woodblock printing, calligraphy, drawing, papercutting, and paper folding have been used in Chinese New Year celebrations for centuries. These ancient art forms are still practiced by amateurs and professionals and appreciated worldwide.

Painting

The earliest Chinese paintings were first done on walls, then silk and paper. Although ancient work often featured people, nature was a favorite theme. For example, pictures showed mist-covered mountains that seemed to touch the sky, suggesting that they must be sacred places. The bamboo, a plant signifying strength and often displayed during the Chinese New Year, has been a frequent subject of paintings.[4]

Paintings could be large, sometimes 7 feet tall, and folded up into vertical or horizontal scrolls. Other pictures were small enough to decorate a fan.

One 17-inch-tall work, done in ink on paper, was painted in A.D. 1350 by artist Wu Zhen. Another painting, *Spring Festival Along the River*, was created around the same time by Zhang Zeduan. Over 17 feet tall, the painting shows storytellers, shopkeepers and other townspeople during the Chinese New Year holiday.[5]

Nature is a favorite theme among Chinese artists.

Woodblock Printing

Woodblock printing is the ancient art of carving pictures, designs, or words into a block of wood and pressing it onto paper using paint in one or more colors. The Chinese invented this form of printing in approximately A.D. 750.

In the beginning, figures were drawn simply. Sometimes artists drew black outlines and colored them in afterward. Years later, brightly colored inks were applied during the printing process and designs became more complicated. By the 1600s, Chinese printers were using soft watercolors to make their work look like painting.[6]

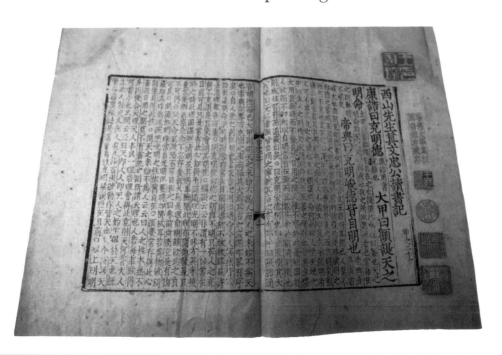

The Chinese invented woodblock printing centuries ago.

In about A.D. 960, Chinese New Year pictures were printed from wood blocks. They began with Door God images and later featured characters from well-known stories. Over time, artists created pictures of birds, flowers, nature scenes, and children at play.

Symbolism is often used on New Year prints to express wishes for the year ahead. A peach and a crane, for example, symbolize hope for a long life.

Calligraphy

Calligraphy is the art of forming beautiful letters with a brush and ink. Brushes have a narrow point and may be made from animal fur or whiskers. The five types of calligraphic writing—seal, clerical, standard, running, and cursive—may express an artist's mood and personality.

Calligraphy evolved after paper was invented in China in approximately A.D. 200. The art took years of study and training. The best Chinese calligraphers grew famous, and their work is highly valued. The most famous artist was Wang Xizhi, who lived during A.D. 303–361.

During the Chinese New Year season, many homes have hanging scrolls with holiday messages

Calligraphy is a form of writing. These are some of the tools that are used.

written in calligraphy. These scrolls may frame doorways or decorate living rooms.[7]

Papercutting and Paper Folding

Although paper was invented in China in A.D. 105, it was too precious to use for decorating. The

The Invention of Paper

The paper used today is based on the discoveries of Ts'ai Lun during the Han dynasty (202 B.C.–A.D. 220). He disliked using silk and bamboo, the only materials available for writing in approximately A.D. 105. He tried to find something better, and eventually learned that the inner bark of a mulberry tree could be torn into fibers, ground into pulp with water and bamboo fibers, and flattened into a sheet. Over one century later, a plant called hemp was used for fiber as well.[8]

Chinese art of papercutting—cutting thin paper into designs and pictures—began in approximately A.D. 300. Using colored paper began sometime during the Tang dynasty (from A.D. 618–906).

Papercutting requires scissors or sharp knives. Paper-cutters may follow a pattern or work freehand to create butterflies, birds, animals, plants, flowers, scenes from daily life, or of legendary stories and characters.

People hang papercuts on doorways during the Chinese New Year to bring good luck. Designs may also decorate windows. Red and gold are widely used colors at this time.[9]

To celebrate the Year of the Horse, this merchant hung a red banner over the door.

Paper folding is another ancient Chinese art form. Its beginnings are unclear, but skillfully folding paper into birds and animals probably began in A.D. 300. Paper-folded creations are also used to decorate homes during the Chinese New Year season. Paper flowers and paper lanterns are created during this time too.[10]

Music, Dance, Drama

During the Chinese New Year holiday, entertainers from all over the world dance, sing, play musical instruments, and present plays. Chinese New Year parades are especially known for their lion and dragon dances.

Lion dances are an important part of Chinese New Year. This lion dance took place in Hong Kong.

Lion dances began in Chinese villages during the Ming dynasty (A.D. 1368–1644). They were done especially for the Chinese New Year to chase away evil spirits and bring good luck. The dance is performed to loud drums, gongs, cymbals, and bells. Two dancers conduct acrobatic movements beneath a bright costume of long yellow fur. One dancer is in the front, the other is in the back.

Over time, it became customary for lion dancers to strut by shops and other businesses to bring good luck to people in the new year. The dancers may receive "lucky money" in return.

The dragon dance is another favorite among holiday audiences. Although dragons are frightening beings in many cultures, they symbolize strength and good fortune in Chinese folklore. The dragon dance began in approximately 1200.

In the dancc, "dragons" may be 20 or 30 feet long. Many dancers work together under a cloth- or paper-covered bamboo frame of gold, green, or red, moving the huge creation to loud music. There may be nine to twenty-four sections of the dragon carried by members of the performing group. The largest dragon dance in the world today is held at San Francisco's annual Chinese New Year Parade.[11]

This is a dog costume for the traditional dragon dance.

The *yangko* is a type of folk dance seen mostly in northern China during the New Year season. Dancers portray ancient goblins and other figures while singing their stories. The dance began in ancient times when farmers took breaks from their work in the fields. Centuries later, in 770–476 B.C., the *yangko* was performed at festivals.

Stilt-walking, another form of dance, is performed on tall, thin wooden sticks ranging from over one foot to five feet high. Dancers wear colorful makeup and costumes while dramatizing characters from operas and folktales. Moving to lively music, they do somersaults, jumps, splits, handstands, and full-circle turns on their stilts.[12]

On New Year's Day in Beijing, China, boys and girls walk on wooden stilts that are over one yard long. They dance, visit homes, and present a play on the stilts. They also perform acrobatics that include jumping on one leg and making turns.[13]

Acrobatics have been performed in China for centuries and led to a type of theater called Beijing Opera, also known as the Peking Opera. Featured worldwide during the Chinese New Year season, the show combines acting, singing, dancing, and acrobatics. Stories might be about gods, heroes, war, or families.

Chinese opera is still popular today. This actor is in full costume.

An orchestra of loud drums, gongs, cymbals, and special reed and stringed instruments accompanies the entertainers, who wear beautiful costumes and masks or painted faces to help them portray their characters. They sing in loud voices, because the shows were traditionally held outdoors. For that reason, and for easier traveling from one place to another, sets are not used. Dancers often use fans, long ribbons, feathers, scarves, swords, and umbrellas to help them express stories.[14]

Poetry

A form of poetry connected with the Chinese New Year festival is spring couplets, one to five lines of successive verse. Couplets express hopeful wishes for the new year. The fabric or paper they are written on are usually decorated with good luck symbols. The couplet below, which many people believe was the first ever written, was by Emperor Meng Zhang in approximately A.D. 900, during the Tang dynasty.

> *The New Year brings in overflowing*
> *good fortune,*
>
> *The great festival is named*
> *Everlasting Spring.*

Today's couplets for the Chinese New Year may be simple greetings, such as "May all your wishes be fulfilled."[15]

Horticulture and Flower Arranging

Horticulture, the science or art of growing flowers, plants, fruits, and vegetables, plays an important role in Chinese New Year celebrations. Beginning on about December 26, outdoor flower markets are set up in Chinese communities with rows of budding plants for sale. The idea is for flowers to reach full bloom by Chinese New Year's Eve. It is believed that the amount of blossom that opens in a house measures the wealth the family will have in the next twelve months, so timing a plant's growth is important.

The most common holiday arrangements are called the "Three Friends of the Cold Season"—the Japanese apricot, the bamboo, and the pine. These plants are grouped with flowers symbolizing good fortune. The narcissus, for example, represents wealth.[16]

Homes and businesses are filled with plants and flowers during the New Year season. Although they are mostly decorative, many have special meanings. Red flowers are popular choices, especially the peony, which symbolizes good fortune. More flowers are listed below.

The Money Tree is often seen in homes, restaurants, and hotel lobbies during the Chinese New Year celebration. The plant is an offering to

Flower	Meaning
Narcissus	Good fortune and prosperity
Camellia	Spring
Evergreen	Strength
Peach	Long life
Kumquat	Gold and prosperity
Plum blossom	Friendship [17]

The camellia symbolizes the spring season.

the God of Wealth, with the hope that money will be plentiful in the new year.

Money Trees are usually small citrus trees or bare twigs. Decorating them is an ancient Chinese custom and may have influenced the trimming of Christmas trees.

Money Trees are made by cutting a branch and putting it in a bowl filled with rice grains. Almonds and walnuts are placed over the rice. Gold and silver paper and artificial flowers may decorate the branches.

A paper figure of a man with five coins floating above him is put at the top of the tree. He holds a scroll inscribed with good wishes, such as "May the entire family find joy" or "May the four seasons be peaceful."

Cut-outs of coins strung with red ribbons or strings are hung on branches. Various seeds and nuts may also trim the tree, along with paper-folded birds, deer, and horses.[18]

◆ ◆ ◆ ◆

By enhancing various art forms, the New Year holiday has influenced the Chinese culture and others as well. To the Chinese people, however, the festival is mostly about reunion, remembering, and rejoicing.

To celebrate the Year of the Monkey in 2004, these girls get ready for their performance in a Chinese New Year celebration in Seattle, Washington.

Friends and Family

Although the Chinese New Year is a joyous celebration, it is mostly about reuniting with friends and family and giving thanks. The holiday officially begins on Chinese New Year's Eve, but preparations start weeks before. People shop, clean, and cook to get ready for the most spiritual time of the year.

Most rituals sprang from ancient customs and beliefs. But not everyone celebrates Chinese New Year the same way. Some people who have immigrated to other countries do not celebrate the holiday at all. In China though, especially in the northern regions, many practices have stayed traditional.[1]

Getting Ready

In many homes, food shopping starts early, before stores run out of needed supplies. Much of the cooking begins ahead of time too. Many families follow a tradition of boiling dumplings together.[2]

Homes are cleaned thoroughly, partly to throw away any bad luck that gathered during the past year. All cleaning must be finished by Chinese New Year's Eve so that good luck for the new year is not accidentally thrown away. It is believed that cutting with scissors during the Chinese New Year is like cutting into good fortune, so many people get their hair cut before the holiday.[3]

Food jars may have pasted strips of red paper on them with symbols meaning, "May this jar always be full." People buy long red paper for writing Chinese New Year sayings that express wishes for good health, good luck, and a long life. These papers are hung on both sides of a doorway. Some red papers are bought with sayings already written on them.[4]

Chinese New Year greetings adorn a door in Singapore.

Colorful, beautifully printed greeting cards are sent about a week before the holiday to all friends and family so no one feels left out. The cards contain good wishes for the new year and character symbols representing luck, success, and longevity.[5] The tradition of sending greeting cards began in approximately 200 B.C.

Flowers symbolize the coming of spring and hope for the new year. They also brighten and decorate homes and are given as gifts. People shop at flower markets before the Chinese New Year to buy their favorites.[6]

Before and during the holiday, everyone is especially polite to each other. It is believed that rudeness will bring bad luck to the family in the new year. Scolding children is also avoided. It is said that if one cries on the holiday, one will cry all year, so people try to be happy.

Any disagreements or arguments must be settled before the Chinese New Year begins.[7] All debts must be paid by then, too.[8]

The Kitchen God

The Kitchen God, also known as Zaowangye, or Zhang, is the most important divine being in traditional Chinese homes. He is believed to observe the good and evil done by everyone in a household. A picture of him, or his name on paper, is hung over the kitchen stove, considered the center of family life.

It is believed that about a week before the New Year, the Kitchen God travels to Heaven and makes his report to the God of Heaven, the Jade Emperor, about what happened on Earth during the year. On this day, in the afternoon or early evening, the eldest male of a household conducts a ceremony to give the Kitchen God a farewell celebration. It is customary to smear the god's mouth with honey or molasses, either to "sweeten his tongue" so he will say good things about the family, or close his mouth so nothing is said at all. The god's picture is then removed from the wall and burned "to send his spirit to the heavens."[9]

The Big Night

Finally, it is Chinese New Year's Eve. A new picture of the Kitchen God is hung on the wall over the stove to watch the family for another year. Homes are spotless. Dinner tables are set. The food is prepared.

People are dressed in new or their best clothing as they welcome their relatives. Wearing black and white is avoided because both are connected to death and sadness in the Chinese culture. Hair is freshly washed, because shampooing on the holiday is forbidden—good luck might be rinsed away.

The Chinese Language

Mandarin is the most widely spoken language in China. In places such as Hong Kong, however, Cantonese is the main language. The languages differ mostly in pronunciation and grammar. Both languages use the same Chinese characters in their writing.[10]

Common New Year greetings are *Sun Nien Fai Lok*, which means "Happy New Year," and *Gong Hay, Fat Choy*, meaning "Wishing you happiness and wealth."[11]

The Ancestral Altar

The ancestral altar stands in the living room. Pictures of deceased relatives are nearby. On Chinese New Year's Eve, flowers, food, and candles are placed on the altar for the ancestors, to show respect to them and to unify the family.

Following the custom of allowing one's elders to eat first, many families bring the Chinese New Year's Eve meal to the altar. The food is a way of giving thanks, because people believe that the family's good luck is connected to their ancestors watching over them. The eldest male says a prayer for the family.[12]

The Big Meal

In most homes, the Chinese New Year's Eve dinner is the most important meal of the year. It begins when every family member is present at the table. There is a place setting for anyone unable to come home for dinner that night, symbolizing their presence even though they may be far away. No chipped or cracked plates are used, because a chip

Altars can be set up in homes or temples, such as this one, to honor deceased family members.

means that something is eating into a person's fortune.

Although meals may depend on a family's preferences, some dishes are usually included on the menu. Several round dishes, such as dumplings and fish cakes, are served, because the word for "round" and "reunion" sound the same in Chinese.

Dinner may start with soup, a bird's nest soup for long life and a shark fin soup for prosperity. A dish called *jai choy* contains vegetables that promise good fortune, such as snow peas for luck and prosperity.[13]

Chicken or turkey is served whole, signifying a favorable start and finish to the new year. "No New Year's dinner was complete without a whole chicken," says Grace Young, a chef and cookbook author, about her family's Chinese New Year celebrations in San Francisco. Long noodles, long-grain rice, and long Chinese string beans, all symbolizing longevity, were also served. Noodles are not cut for easier eating as that would represent a shortened life.[14]

Dessert is usually fresh fruit, especially oranges and tangerines. Because they resemble gold coins, these items signify prosperity.[15]

Families create and then enjoy big feasts for their Chinese New Year celebration.

A circular snack tray, called the "Tray of Togetherness," is served for a sweet new year. It has eight sections, because in Chinese, "eight" sounds like "to grow." Each section has treats such as candied melons for good health, peanuts for a long life, melon seeds—dyed red—symbolizing joy and wealth, lychee nuts representing strong family ties, sugared coconut slices for togetherness, and plums, kumquats, and red dates.

Niangao, the sweet, sticky rice cake, is usually served. Eating it symbolizes the wish "to rise in rank or wealth year after year." Other New Year treats are thin, yellow "egg roll" cookies and "cow tails," which are fried, braided dough.

Families make sure there is leftover food to symbolize that there will be enough in the new year. Since it is traditionally forbidden to cook on Chinese New Year's Day, extra food is also necessary.[16]

Waiting for the New Year

After dinner, adults give children "lucky money" in red envelopes—*lai-see* in Cantonese or *hong bao* in Mandarin. The envelope has designs in gold and holiday wishes written on it. The family then gathers together for a ceremony to bid farewell to the year. The younger people bow to their elders. Aside from showing respect, the custom represents the hope that one's parents will live to an old age.[17]

In the Chinese culture, noise represents life, joy, and happiness, and the use of firecrackers is

Children and adults may receive red envelopes filled with money during Chinese New Year.

part of many celebrations. Although firecrackers are forbidden in Beijing, the capital of the People's Republic of China, and other large cities, they are still used in smaller regions.[18]

Many people follow the ancient ritual of staying awake on Chinese New Year's Eve. It is thought that going to bed early takes away from one's happiness and is considered bad luck. People believe that by letting children stay awake for as long as they can, their elders' lives will be lengthened.

During the night, families chat, play games, and watch special holiday programs on television. Telling ghost stories, or any talk about death, is forbidden.[19]

Bells ring at midnight, signaling the start of a new year. Windows and doors may be left open to let the old year out and to let good spirits enter the house.

Coins threaded with colored string and arranged to resemble a dragon may be put near children's beds to protect them during the new year. Lucky money is often placed under their pillows.[20]

The Big Day

In the morning, everyone greets each other happily, glad that they survived the night unharmed from evil spirits. The first person one meets and the first words one hears are important, because they predict the type of luck one may expect during the year. Children bow to their parents and grandparents, offer them soup or tea, and wish them good health.

After the Big Day

The days after Chinese New Year's Day have their own customs and traditions. For example, people bring oranges, tangerines, or *niangao* when visiting family or friends. Lucky money envelopes are also brought when going to a home where there are children.

- Parties and dinners with friends are often held on the second night of the New Year.
- People usually stay home on the third day because it is considered an unlucky day. They get some needed rest.
- People "welcome the gods" early in the morning of the fourth day with offerings of fruit and other treats.
- On the fifth day, everyone in the house rises early while dirt is gathered throughout the house, placed in a pan, and taken out into the street.
- People visit friends and neighbors or stay home on the sixth day.

In downtown Seattle, Washington, in 2004, dancers with the Mak Fai Kung Fu Club perform a dragon dance.

- Only noodles, for a long life, and vegetables are catcn on thc scvcnth day.
- If the eighth day is sunny, people predict a good harvest for the year.
- The birthday of the Jade Emperor is celebrated on the ninth day.
- People often give parties for friends and family on the tenth and eleventh days.
- The twelfth day is the last day for New Year greetings.
- Year-round foods are served on the thirteenth day.
- On the fourteenth day, preparations begin for the last days of the New Year season, called the Lantern Festival.
- The Lantern Festival begins on the fifteenth night.[21]

The Lantern Festival

The Lantern Festival begins with the first full moon of the Chinese New Year and is the last of the holiday rituals. Public viewing of beautifully decorated lanterns, representing the brightness of spring, has been a favorite pastime for centuries.[22]

Lanterns are made from thin bamboo or wooden frames and are usually round, square, or oblong. They are covered with paper or silk, although sheepskin or glass may be used. The paper is painted or has designs cut into them. Silk fabrics are painted or have sewn-on designs. Decorations may have themes about animals, dragons, flowers, or people. Other lantern pictures are scenes from well-known Chinese folktales. Red, black, and yellow are the colors often used in lantern designs.

Lanterns are hung on a wall, placed on a stand, or hung on a pole.[23] Children carry lanterns during Lantern Festival parades. Contests may be held to see who has the best one.

Lantern Festival celebrations also include folk-song and dance performances, such as the dragon dance and lion dance. Other kinds of entertainment are clown acts, puppet shows, stilt-walking, juggling, storytelling, wrestling contests, and gymnastic events.

During the Lantern Festival, it is customary to eat *yuanxiao*, a sweet-tasting ball of rice that means "first full moon" in Chinese. It is usually eaten in a soup called *tanguan*, or "first soup." *Yuanxiao* is usually stuffed with meat, fish, or sweet fillings, such as honey and white grapes.[24]

◆ ◆ ◆ ◆

Customs and how or if they are practiced depend on where people live and their family

The Lantern Festival is the last day of the Chinese New Year. Lanterns of all shapes and sizes are on display. These lanterns, in Shanghai, China, signified the year 2005 as the Year of the Rooster.

Lantern Riddle Parties

Lantern riddle parties are sometimes held on the fifteenth night of the Chinese New Year holiday. People try to solve riddles that are pasted on the outside of lanterns, and whoever succeeds wins a prize. Newspapers, magazines, and department stores also offer riddles for people to solve.

Below are two lantern riddles.

Two small boats, five guests in each,
sail on land but never on water.
Busy during the daytime,
anchored at night.
Answer: A pair of shoes.

This guy runs fast but cannot stand.
People ride this horse who never eats grass.
Answer: A bicycle.[25]

traditions. In New York City, for example, some people are unaware that haircutting is considered unlucky on Chinese New Year. Others in the area follow that belief very closely.

Chinese New Year celebrations are mainly about family and friends. But the holiday's signs and symbols help unite people and add great joy to the festival.

The peach
represents
longevity.

Signs and Symbols

On doors and windows throughout Chinese communities, signs and symbols are displayed to greet the new year. These festive decorations bring cheer and meaning to the season and strengthen ties to an ancient culture.

The Peach

Of all the plants and flowers connected with Chinese New Year, the peach is considered the most special. It represents longevity and it grew in China first.

In ancient times, a bunch of peach blossoms was placed above people's front doors to chase away evil spirits. Today they are used mostly as decorations.[1]

Door God Posters

Door God posters are hung on both sides of doorways during the New Year season. Many people believe that the gods have special powers that can protect everyone living in the homes they are guarding.

Door God posters often feature two generals who served Emperor Taizong during the Tang dynasty (A.D. 618–907). When the emperor was ill and had a bad dream about a ghost, the generals stood outside his door to guard him. Knowing he was protected, the ruler slept well.

But after a few nights, he did not want to bother the men anymore. He ordered two paintings, one of each general. When the pictures were completed, they were put on the emperor's door.

As people heard this story, they wanted protection too. They made their own paintings of the guards and hung them on their doors. The tradition has continued ever since.

Other Door Gods are the mythical brothers Shen-shu and Yu-lu. Pictures of them were traditionally on peachwood plates, also called peachwood charms, with each man's name written on them. The plates were hung on both sides of doorways so they could chase away evil spirits.

Both stories explain why Door God posters are always sold in pairs. Today they are made in factories, in time for the Chinese New Year holiday.[2]

Spring Couplets

Spring couplets are written on long columns of bright red paper. They are hung on both sides of doorways to homes, shops, and offices. The verses express hope for the new year, such as "When you attract wealth, precious goods follow."

A third strip of paper is often placed above a doorway. It may have pictures symbolizing prosperity, such as fish, because the Chinese word for fish and plenty are the same.[3]

Spring couplets may also be written on square red papers. All spring couplets are hung by Chinese New Year's Eve.

Door Streamers

Door streamers are paper cuts that have patterns cut from pink, green, blue, or yellow paper. Their lower edges are shredded into tassels. Red paper is not used for door streamers so that attention will not be taken away from the spring couplets.

Door streamers portray flowers, birds, and insects. They also have characters written on them symbolizing fortune, wealth, happiness, or other hopeful wishes. The streamers brighten neighborhoods and add to the holiday feeling. In northern China, green door streamers are called "spring leaves."[4]

The *Fu* Sign

In homes, shops, and offices, red signs have the Chinese word *fu* written on them in calligraphy. *Fu* means good luck and happiness. The signs are made of paper or cloth.

The practice of hanging the *fu* character began with an old story from the Ming dynasty. One day, while Emperor Hung Wu (1368–1398) was traveling through his territory, he saw signs on many of the doors that made fun of his wife. He became so angry that he put *fu* papers on doors that did not have the insulting signs. By the next morning, the houses without the *fu* symbol were destroyed.[5]

Pictures of Bats

Because the Chinese word for a "bat" is pronounced *fu* but is spelled differently in Chinese, pictures of bats are familiar symbols of good luck and happiness. These signs are seen throughout the year but especially during the Chinese New Year season.

A picture of two bats is a double wish for luck. Five bats represent the Five Blessings: a long life, a pure life, riches, health, and a "natural death." A red bat is especially lucky, because the color also symbolizes good fortune.[6]

Red Envelopes of "Lucky Money"

Lucky money packed in red envelopes symbolizes good luck for the giver and the receiver. It is customary for people to accept the envelopes with three kneeling bows. Envelopes stay closed until the giver and receiver part company.[7]

The Almanac

Almanacs date back to ancient times and were among the first books published by Chinese emperors. They are still written each year and are among the most widely sold books in China.

Almanacs include the solar and lunar calendars for the new year. They give the best

These two girls in San Francisco, California, are making lanterns from red envelopes.

dates to plant crops and offer weather predictions. The book also supplies other information, such as lucky days. It is consulted by many Chinese people throughout the world before they plan big events. Almanacs are often given as Chinese New Year gifts.[8]

The Chinese Calendar

Although the Gregorian calendar has been in use for many years, the Chinese calendar is still referred to by millions of people. It is important for planning holidays and other special occasions.

The calendar represents the passing of one year and welcoming another. It also symbolizes an invention that has lasted longer than any other culture's. Like the almanac, calendars are popular Chinese New Year gifts.

Astrological Signs

Each Chinese New Year is linked to one of the twelve zodiac animals. The following list includes the animals and the character traits they portray. These creatures are often used as signs and decorations throughout the year they represent.

Rat	Imaginative, charming, generous, cunning
Ox	Leader, dependable, honest, patient
Tiger	Sensitive, rebellious, adventurous, energetic
Rabbit	Pleasant, gentle, artistic, cautious
Dragon	Ambitious, daring, gifted, confident
Snake	Wise, charming, romantic, powerful

Horse   Hardworking, intelligent, friendly, athletic

Sheep   Compassionate, artistic, calm, generous

Monkey   Intelligent, polite, ambitious, funny

Rooster   Clever, articulate, honest, hardworking

Dog   Dependable, fair, intelligent, brave

Pig   Loyal, honest, courageous, generous[9]

◆ ◆ ◆ ◆

The signs and symbols mentioned in this chapter are seen in Chinese communities throughout the world. They represent old customs that are still meaningful, and unify a large population during a special time of year.

Find Your Sign!

Find your Chinese astrological sign by looking up your birth year on the chart below.

Then read the personality traits listed for your sign on pages 77 and 78.

Check the signs of your family and friends too. Note that twelve years pass before a sign is repeated.

Rat	1936	1948	1960	1972	1984	1996
Ox	1937	1949	1961	1973	1985	1997
Tiger	1938	1950	1962	1974	1986	1998
Rabbit	1939	1951	1963	1975	1987	1999
Dragon	1940	1952	1964	1976	1988	2000
Snake	1941	1953	1965	1977	1989	2001
Horse	1942	1954	1966	1978	1990	2002
Sheep	1943	1955	1967	1979	1991	2003
Monkey	1944	1956	1968	1980	1992	2004
Rooster	1945	1957	1969	1981	1993	2005
Dog	1946	1958	1970	1982	1994	2006
Pig	1947	1959	1971	1983	1995	2007

In 2006, in San Francisco, California, this little girl waits to perform a lion dance.

The Chinese New Year Today

Although the worldwide Chinese population recognizes January 1 as the official first day of the year, millions of people celebrate the Chinese New Year season. Many of the customs and rituals established long ago are still practiced. Some people may only share a big meal with their family, or watch a grand parade. Still, they are continuing a valuable tradition.

People who have immigrated to other countries may find it difficult to participate in all of the holiday's festivities. "Some people do not have time to celebrate," said Mavis Ngo, who lived in China and is now in San Francisco. "They have jobs to go to. It is not like in China, where offices, factories, and schools are closed for two weeks. If the holiday falls on the weekend here, people can enjoy it. Otherwise, many put work or school first."[1]

Food preparation for the holiday has changed, too. Because most people lack time to create big meals with difficult recipes, many foods are bought in stores and markets. Dumplings are sold ready-made. Piles of cellophane-wrapped *niangao* are in Chinese markets before the holiday.[2] Some items are ordered frozen, then thawed or microwaved before mealtime.

Other changes involve firecrackers. For over a decade, they have been banned in many large cities to keep people safe from possible injury. Today, event planners hire professional fireworks companies for Chinese New Year celebrations.

China's ban may be lifted, though, because people feel it ruins the spirit of the holiday. They miss what firecrackers represent—the traditional noise and the ancient custom of chasing away demons, especially on Chinese New Year's Eve. In the meantime, many people use plastic fireworks to decorate holiday displays, such as Money Trees.

New Year greeting cards are still exchanged, but they are usually mass-produced in factories, not drawn by hand as they were years ago. Spring couplets are manufactured by companies and sold in shops. New Year prints are made in workshops throughout China, where millions of designs are created each year.

Many people send holiday wishes using high-speed technology, such as e-mail. Although ways of communicating have changed, many Chinese New Year festivities have stayed the same. Here is how some regions celebrate this cheerful time.

San Francisco, California

In 1848, when gold was discovered in California mines, thousands of people from China and other countries immigrated to the United States to seek their fortunes. Immigration increased again during the 1860s, when workers were brought from China by the Central Pacific Railroad Company to help build the western portion of America's first transcontinental railroad.[3]

By the 1880s, one fourth of San Francisco's population was Chinese. To share their culture, neighborhoods had Chinese New Year parades.

Streets in Chinatown in San Francisco, California, are decorated for Chinese New Year.

People carried flags, banners, and lanterns. They banged on drums and lit firecrackers. These small nighttime parades were held every year.

In 1953, Henry K. Wong, an American businessman, wanted one large parade for San

Francisco. He hoped to familiarize more Americans with the Chinese culture and to attract more shoppers and tourists to Chinatown. Getting support from the San Francisco community brought Chinese New Year events that included Chinese art shows, dancing, a martial arts exhibition, music, and a big parade.

The following year, a Miss Chinatown beauty contest became part of the festivities. In 1958, the program became a nationwide event called "Miss Chinatown, USA," allowing women from every state to compete.[4]

Today the parade, officially known as the Southwest Airlines Chinese New Year Festival and Parade, is the largest celebration of Asian culture outside of China. Millions of people attend the event and watch it on television.

The parade has over fifty floats carrying figures of legendary gods and many entertainers in bright costumes. Marching bands, stilt-walkers, lion dancers, acrobats, and firecrackers put on a lively show. People carry colorful flags, banners, and lanterns. Drummers make lots of noise to chase away evil spirits.

The main attraction is a 201-foot-long golden dragon with brightly lit bulbs. Made of bamboo, its body is divided into twenty-nine parts and needs over one hundred people to carry it through San Francisco's streets.[5]

There is also a lion dance. Fourteen-year-old Daniel Lang is one of the dancers. He belongs to a sports club in the city and parades with members of the San Francisco Police Department. "It is a lot of fun," Daniel said. "I am the front of the lion. My friends and family see me on TV! Next to getting red envelopes from my parents and relatives, it is the best part of the holiday."[6]

The city also has the country's largest flower market, which is several blocks long. People enjoy strolling through it on New Year's Eve while waiting for midnight.

New York City, New York

For safety reasons, firecrackers have been banned in New York since 1997. People may, however, receive a permit from their local fire department or hire professional companies for an event.[7]

Bundles of artificial firecrackers can be bought as decorations. Some light up and make loud noises.

One week before the Chinese New Year, flower markets are set up in New York's Chinatown. There is also a Chinese New Year Gala held in Madison Square Garden. An international cast of dancers,

Many people
in New York
come out
to watch the
festivities
during the lion
dance parade.

musicians, and singers performs a big show that presents the Chinese culture.[8]

The Chinatown Lunar New Year Parade and Festival has colorful floats, marching bands, fireworks, a lion dance, musicians, magicians, and acrobats. Before the first parade several years ago, New York's Chinese communities had local, smaller celebrations. Then leaders such as Steven Tin, director of the Chinatown Events Society, wanted New York to present the elaborate festival San Francisco has. The result is a larger program that attracts a bigger audience.

The Dragon Parade, marking the end of the Chinese New Year celebration, is an all-day event. Many groups perform authentic and ancient dances, including the famous dragon dance. Entertainers move beneath the creature, twisting and turning its long silk body and controlling its blinking eyes.[9]

Cara Chang, a sixth-grader living with her family in Chinatown, enjoys these festivities and commented on how she and her family observe the Chinese New Year season. "We celebrate the holiday like many families," she said. "I help my parents clean our apartment. We decorate it with special signs written in Chinese."

Cara continued:

I cut my hair before the New Year. Some of my friends do not, but in my family it is important. We invite relatives and everyone gives me and my older sister red envelopes. I save mine.

At dinner, we eat chicken, turkey, and ham. I stay up all night with my family on New Year's Eve. We talk and watch television. We also go to the big parade and see the lion dance.

I try to be very polite this time of year. I believe there is good luck.[10]

Hong Kong

Beautiful flower markets and sparkling neon lights on tall office buildings begin the Chinese New Year season in Hong Kong. The big celebration is the International Chinese New Year Parade, attended by over three hundred thousand people.

The parade has beautiful floats, marching bands, dragon and lion dancers, and other performers from all over the world. There is also a glittering fireworks display over Victoria Harbor.[11]

One tourist described her visit to Hong Kong during the Chinese New Year season:

It was exciting and fun! In the hotel lobby, men danced under a huge dragon costume, two in the front and two in the back.

Musicians banged on enormous, ancient-looking drums and cymbals. Acrobats wore brightly colored outfits. Marchers threw candy. Red silk banners with gold lettering hung on the walls. The whole thing was very festive, perfect for a New Year celebration![12]

A young American businessman living in Hong Kong for part of the year said this about the two-week festival:

> The Chinese New Year is the big holiday here in Hong Kong. Businesses, schools, and factories close for about two weeks. There are parades with lion dances, and the family meals are very festive. Everyone decorates their homes and office buildings, mostly in red and gold. The streets look beautiful. Money in red envelopes is exchanged between people to symbolize good luck and good fortune. As a foreigner, there isn't much celebration, but you get to see the Chinese participating in their culture. And you get a few days off to rest![13]

Taiwan

Taiwan is an island in the South China Sea, about ninety miles off China's coast. Most Taiwanese are Chinese whose ancestors immigrated to the island.

To bring luck for the new year, the Taiwanese enjoy a dish called the "Five Blessings for the New Year." It represents long life, wealth, peace, wisdom, and goodness. They may also have fish to symbolize having enough food for the new year, and turnips, which represent good fortune.

Most Taiwanese people follow Buddhism, Taoism, and a local religion that involves worshiping special gods and goddesses. The temples, places of worship, are especially busy during the New Year season, with people praying for good luck and happiness.[14]

Singapore

Located in southeast Asia, Singapore is a small country made up of many islands. About 75 percent of its population is Chinese. On Chinese New Year's Eve in Singapore's Chinatown district, a joyful countdown party is held where people gather to welcome the new year. At midnight, there are booming firecrackers and brilliant fireworks.

A New Year's Day parade has beautifully decorated floats and a dragon dance. The "dragon" is supported by twenty boys on roller skates. Using sticks to carry the dragon, the boys perform athletic movements to make the creature jump, spin, and rise up.

In Singapore, people watched a fireworks display during the first night of Chinese New Year.

Street bazaars, with over four hundred stalls selling food, flowers, and other merchandise, are open throughout the holiday. Chinese cultural shows are held nightly, featuring performances by local and international entertainers.[15]

Vietnam

Tet Nguyen Dan is the Lunar New Year holiday in Vietnam. *Tet*, as it is mostly referred to, was brought to Vietnam by the Chinese when China ruled the nation.

Tet is celebrated almost the same way as Chinese New Year. Although firecrackers are illegal in Vietnam, noisy musical instruments are used to frighten away evil spirits. Parades feature a unicorn that chases demons and symbolizes strength in the Vietnamese culture. A favorite holiday dish is *banh chung*, a steamed sticky rice cake with pork stuffing wrapped in banana leaves.

One difference between the Chinese and Vietnamese lunar holidays is that the Vietnamese replaced the Ox, Rabbit, and Sheep in the Chinese calendar with the Buffalo, Cat, and Goat.[16]

Korea

Koreans celebrate the Lunar New Year in much the same way as the Chinese. Most businesses are closed, and people visit their families. Although some customs are similar, others are different. For example, red is not a special color to Koreans, but to both cultures, honoring parents and ancestors is an important part of the holiday.

On Lunar New Year's Eve, Koreans sit up all night to "defend the new year from evil spirits." In Seoul, the country's capital, church bells ring thirty-three times at midnight.

A traditional food eaten for the holiday is *duggook* soup, "for good luck." It is made from rice and contains poultry, meat, pine nuts, and chestnuts.[17]

England

In 2005, about fifty-thousand people crowded into central London, England's capital, for Chinese New Year festivities. There was a Grand Parade, with more than 150 costumed performers, including Beijing Opera singers and stilt-walkers. Elsewhere in the city were dancers from the Chinese Ballet of Beijing, acrobats, dragon and lion dancers, and a martial arts demonstration. There was also a puppet theatre, fireworks displays, and a photography exhibition about early Chinese immigration to London.[18]

New Zealand

Along the waterfront in Wellington, the capital of New Zealand, is the Asian Market. It is especially busy before Chinese New Year, with people selling

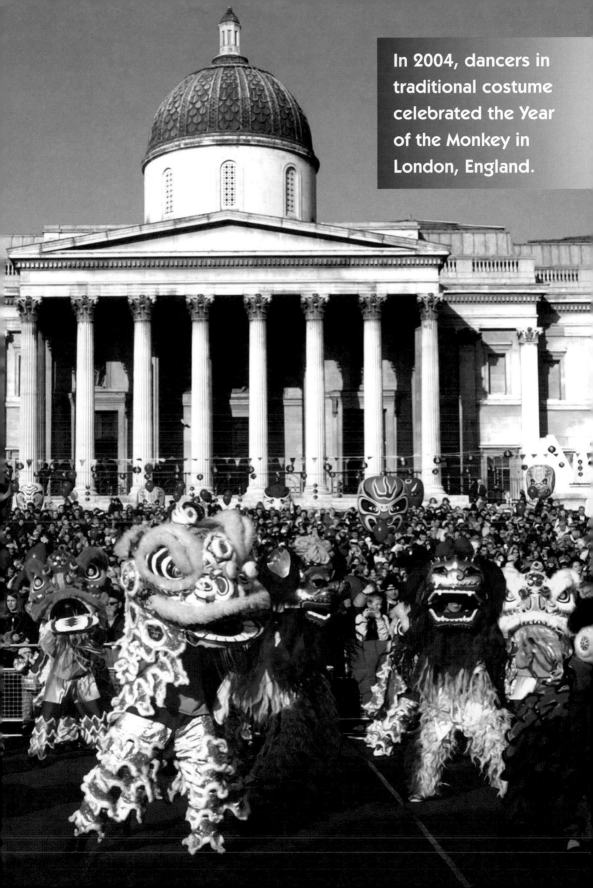

In 2004, dancers in traditional costume celebrated the Year of the Monkey in London, England.

Chinese groceries, specially prepared food, Chinese art, holiday crafts, and clothes. There are also cooking demonstrations, Chinese painting demonstrations, and storytelling.

During the holiday, dragon dancers lead a parade of colorfully decorated floats. Representatives from cultural organizations and the government, including Wellington's mayor, join the marchers. Featured as well are visiting entertainers, such as the China Acrobatic Circus. There are also drummers, stilt-walkers, and an impressive fireworks display, in which red is the main color flashing across the nighttime sky.[19]

❖ ❖ ❖ ❖

Chinese New Year celebrations are held elsewhere, too, such as in Los Angeles, California; Honolulu, Hawaii; Thailand, Cambodia; and Japan. Chinese people have made homes throughout the world, where they have shared their traditions and glorious culture. In doing so, their festival has become an international gift for everyone to enjoy.

The Chinese New Year celebrates time, but not only by recording its passage. Aside from marking the beginning of a new year, the season is a time to hope for the future. It is a time to honor the past by remembering those who came before, and in commemorating centuries of history. It is a time to acknowledge the present by appreciating family and friends. It is a time to soothe hurt feelings and wish others well. Sun Nien Fai Lok—Happy New Year!*

* Cantonese dialect. In the Mandarin dialect, one would say Xin Nian Kuai Le.

Create a Paper Lantern

What you will need:

- ✔ construction paper, any color
- ✔ ruler
- ✔ pencil
- ✔ scissors
- ✔ crayons or markers
- ✔ clear tape

Directions:

1 Fold a piece of construction paper in half lengthwise.

2 Measure, and lightly mark with a pencil, a 1½-inch border on the two short sides. Measure, and lightly mark with a pencil, a 1-inch border on the long open side.

3 With a pencil, lightly mark 1-inch-wide lines from the fold to the border across the paper lengthwise. Cut on each line from the fold to the border. (You will be cutting off every other strip, make sure you have enough lines to leave the borders on the short sides.)

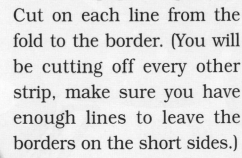

4 Starting with the second strip, cut it off at the border. Do this for every other strip. Do not cut the border or the end strips.

5 Open the paper. If you wish, use crayons or markers to decorate the lantern. Bend and round out the short sides. Tape the two short sides together.

6 Cut a 12-inch-long x 1-inch-wide strip of construction paper. Tape it to the top of the lantern for a handle.

Make more than one lantern for your own Chinese New Year Lantern Festival!

GLOSSARY

ancestor—A person from whom one is descended.

astronomy—The science involving the universe beyond the earth's atmosphere.

calligraphy—A form of script writing made mostly by brush.

commemorate—To honor the memory of someone or something by following an observance.

couplets—Consecutive lines of verse that are usually the same length.

dynasty—A sequence of rulers from the same family or group.

equinox—The time when the sun crosses the earth's equator, making day and night almost the same length all over the earth, occurring about March 21 and September 22.

heritage—Something that comes or belongs to one by birth.

horticulture—The science or art of growing flowers, plants, fruits, and vegetables, especially in a garden, orchard, or nursery.

lunar—Measuring by the moon's revolutions around the earth.

perpetual calendar—A calendar that shows the day of the week on which a given date falls.

ritual—A practice or pattern of behavior regularly performed in a set manner.

solar—Showing time with reference to the sun.

solstice—Either of the two times a year when the sun is at its greatest distance from the equator, occurring about December 22 and June 21.

CHAPTER
NOTES

Chapter 1. A Beast Called Nian

1. Editorial Department of Hong Kong China Tourism Press, *The Grand Spectacle of Chinese New Year Customs* (Hong Kong: Hong Kong China Tourism Press, 1993), p. 12.

Chapter 2. Long Ago and Far Away

1. Richard Louis Edmonds and Richard J. Smith, "China, History," 2005, <http://aolsvc.worldbook. aol.com/wb/> (June 24, 2005).

2. Karen Bellenir, *Religious Holidays and Calendars: An Encyclopedic Handbook* (Detroit: Omnigraphics, Inc., 2004), p. 11.

3. Rita Aero, *Things Chinese* (Garden City, N.Y.: Doubleday, 1980), p. 64.

4. Dorothy Perkins, *Encyclopedia of China: The Essential Reference to China, Its History and Culture* (New York: Facts On File, 1999), pp. 51–52.

5. "Windows to the Universe," *Heng-O and the Twelve Chinese Moons*, 2000, <http://www.windows.ucar. edu/tour/link=/mythology/moon_china.html> (July 27, 2005).

6. "A Walk Through Time/Early Clocks," n.d., <http:// physics.nist.gov/GenInt/Time/early.html> (June 24, 2005).

7. John Matthews, *The Summer Solstice: Celebrating the Journey of the Sun from May Day to Harvest* (Wheaton, Ill.: Quest Books, 2002), pp. 14–15.

8. William C. Hu, *Chinese New Year: Fact and Folklore* (Ann Arbor, Mich.: Ars Ceramica, 1991), pp. 3–6.

9. Editorial Department of Hong Kong China Tourism Press, *The Grand Spectacle of Chinese New Year Customs* (Hong Kong: Hong Kong China Tourism Press, 1993), p. 7.

10. L. Carrington Goodrich, *A Short History of the Chinese People* (Mineola, N.Y.: Dover Publications, 2002), p. 30.

11. Edward L. Shaughnessy, *China, Empire and Civilization* (New York: Oxford University Press, 2000), p. 63.

12. Perkins, p. 630.

13. Hu, pp. 19–28.

14. Rosemary Gong, *Good Luck Life* (New York: Harper-Collins Publishers, 2005), pp. 34–39.

15. Aero, p. 254.

16. Editorial Department of Hong Kong China Tourism Press, p. 7.

17. Hu, p. 17.

18. Hugh B. O'Neill, *Companion to Chinese History* (New York: Facts on File, 1987), pp. 19–21.

19. Bellenir, p. 32.

20. Ibid., pp. 46–48.

21. Ibid., p. 22.

♥ Chapter 3. **The Cultural Importance of the Chinese New Year**

1. Editorial Department of the Hong Kong China Tourism Press, *The Grand Spectacle of Chinese New*

Year Customs (Hong Kong: Hong Kong China Tourism Press, 1993), p. 7.

2. Carol Stepanchuk and Charles Wong, *Mooncakes and Hungry Ghosts: Festivals of China* (San Francisco: China Books, 1991), pp. 18–19.

3. Dorothy Perkins, *Encyclopedia of China: The Essential Reference to China, Its History and Culture* (New York: Facts on File, 1999), p. 105.

4. Patricia B. Ebrey, *The Cambridge Illustrated History of China* (New York: Cambridge University Press, 1996), p. 162.

5. Ibid., p. 145.

6. William C. Hu, *Chinese New Year: Fact and Folklore* (Ann Arbor, Mich.: Ars Ceramica, 1991), pp. 193–196.

7. Edward L. Shaughnessy, ed., *China: Empire and Civilization* (New York: Oxford University Press, 2000), pp. 191–193.

8. Perkins, p. 377.

9. Ibid., p. 378.

10. Rita Aero, *Things Chinese* (Garden City, N.Y.: Doubleday & Company, 1980), p. 185.

11. Stepanchuk and Wong, pp. 37–39.

12. Editorial Department of the Hong Kong China Tourism Press, p. 62.

13. Haga Library, Inc., *Chinese New Year's Day*, n.d., <http://www.hgpho.to/wfest/ch-newyear/c-new year-e.html> (June 21, 2005).

14. Shaughnessy, p. 205.

15. Patricia B. Welch, *Chinese New Year* (New York: Oxford University Press, 1997), pp. 19–22.

16. Ibid., p. 17.

17. Rosemary Gong, *Good Luck Life* (New York: Harper-Collins Publishers, 2005), pp. 11–12.
18. Hu, p. 199.

Chapter 4. **Friends and Family**

1. Personal interview with Ronald S. Chan, June 2005.
2. Rosemary Gong, *Good Luck Life: The Essential Guide to Chinese American Celebration and Culture* (New York: HarperCollins Publishers, 2005), p. 18.
3. Ibid., p. 31.
4. Ibid., p. 9.
5. William C. Hu, *Chinese New Year: Fact and Folklore* (Ann Arbor, Mich.: Ars Ceramica, 1991), p. 261.
6. Patricia B. Welch, *Chinese New Year* (New York: Oxford University Press, 1997), p. 13.
7. Ibid., p. 9.
8. Ibid., p. 31.
9. Carol Stepanchuk and Charles Wong, *Mooncakes and Hungry Ghosts: Festivals of China* (San Francisco: China Books, 1991), pp. 6–7.
10. The Society for Anglo-Chinese Understanding, *Learning Chinese*, n.d., <http://sacu.org/learnlang.html> (August 11, 2005).
11. Gong, p. 15.
12. Ibid., p. 14.
13. Ibid., pp. 16–17.
14. Grace Young, "Soul of a Cook," *More*, vol. 7, October 2004, pp. 160–164.
15. Welch, pp. 14–15.
16. Gong, pp. 18–20.
17. Welch, pp. 37–38.

18. People's Daily Online, "Firecracker Ban May Go Up in Smoke," June 3, 2005, <http://english.people.com.cn/2005/06/03/eng20050603_188265.html> (June 23, 2004).

19. Editorial Department of Hong Kong China Tourism Press, *The Grand Spectacle of Chinese New Year Customs* (Hong Kong: Hong Kong China Tourism Press, 1993), p. 14.

20. Gong, p. 14.

21. Ibid., pp. 27–28.

22. Welch, p. 49.

23. Dorothy Perkins, *Encyclopedia of China, Its History and Culture* (New York: Facts on File, 1999) p. 268.

24. Welch, pp. 52–54.

25. "Lantern Festival 2005, Lighting the Way," *Chinese American Museum, Los Angeles,* 2005, pp. 1–2.

⌄ Chapter 5. Signs and Symbols

1. Wolfram Eberhard, *A Dictionary of Chinese Symbols: Hidden Symbols in Chinese Life and Thought* (New York: Routledge & Kegan Paul, 1986), pp. 227–228.

2. Patricia B. Welch, *Chinese New Year* (New York: Oxford University Press, 1997), pp. 26–27.

3. Ibid., pp. 19–22.

4. Editorial Department of the Hong Kong China Tourism Press, *The Grand Spectacle of Chinese New Year Customs* (Hong Kong: Hong Kong China Tourism Press, 1993), p. 120.

5. Welch, p. 23.

6. Eberhard, p. 32.

7. Welch, pp. 37–38.

8. Edward L. Shaughnessy, *China: Empire and Civilization* (New York: Oxford University Press, 2000), p. 135.

9. Rosemary Gong, *Good Luck Life* (New York: HarperCollins Publishers, 2005), pp. 34–39.

Chapter 6. **The Chinese New Year Today**

1. Personal interview with Mavis Ngo, July 2005.

2. Patricia B. Welch, *Chinese New Year* (New York: Oxford University Press, 1997), p. 36.

3. Andrew Gyory, *Closing the Gate: Race, Politics, and the Chinese Exclusion Act* (Chapel Hill: The University of North Carolina Press, 1998), pp. 6–7.

4. Chiou-LingYeh, "In the Traditions of China and in the Freedom of America: The Making of San Francisco's Chinese New Year Festivals," *American Quarterly*, vol. 56, June 2004, pp. 395–415.

5. *Chinese New Year Parade in San Francisco Chinatown*, 2005, <http://www.sanfranciscochinatown.com/events/chinesenewyearparade.html> (June 20, 2005).

6. Personal interview with Daniel Lang (not his real name), June 2005.

7. Personal interview with Customer Service Representative, New York City Mayor's Citizens Service Center, June 2005.

8. About.com, *Chinese Lunar New Year in New York City: 2005*, 2005, <http://gonyc.about.com/cs/holidays/a/chinesenewyear.htm> (June 20, 2005).

9. Personal interview with Steven Tin, June 2005.

10. Personal interview with Cara Chang, June 2005.

11. Discover Hong Kong, *Chinese New Year Celebrations,* 2005, <http://www.discoverhongkong.com/eng/ heritage/festivals/he_fest_new.jhtml> (June 20, 2005).

12. Personal interview with Geraldine Kule, January 2005.

13. Personal interview with Michael Kule, January 2005.

14. Government Information Office of Taiwan, *Lunar New Year in Taiwan,* 2003, <http://www.gio.gov.tw/ Taiwan-website/5-gp/culture/lunar-NY/> (June 14, 2005).

15. Singapore Tourism Board, *Visit Singapore—Chinese New Year 2005,* n.d., <http://www.visitsingapore. com/cny/origins.htm> (June 20, 2005).

16. Asian-Nation, *Tet, a Celebration of Rebirth,* 2005, <http://www.asian-nation.org/tet.shtml> (June 14, 2005).

17. Life in Korea, *Lunar New Year,* n.d., <http://www. lifeinkorea.com/culture/newyear> (August 3, 2005).

18. Mayor of London—Chinese New Year, *London China Week,* 2005, <http://www.london.gov.uk/mayor/ chinese_ny/chinaweek.jsp> (June 17, 2005).

19. Wellington Chinese New Year Festival, *Festival Program,* 2005, <http://www.chinesenewyear.org. nz> (June 23, 2005).

BOOKS

Asher, Sandy. *China*. New York: Benchmark Books/Marshall Cavendish, 2003.

Flanagan, Alice K. *Chinese New Year Holidays and Festivals*. Mankato, Minn.: Compass Point Books, 2003.

Hoyt-Goldsmith, Diane. *Celebrating Chinese New Year*. New York: Holiday House, 1998.

Simonds, Nina, Leslie Swartz, and the Children's Museum of Boston. *Moonbeams, Dumplings, and Dragon Boats: A Treasury of Chinese Holiday Tales, Activities, and Recipes*. San Diego, Calif.: Harcourt, 2002.

INTERNET ADDRESSES

Celebration of the Chinese New Year
   <http://www.c-c-c.org/chineseculture/festival/
   newyear/newyear.html>

   *Learn more about Chinese New Year at this site from the
   Chinese Culture Center of San Francisco.*

Chinese New Year
   <http://www.kidsdomain.com/holiday/
   chineseny.html>

   Find crafts, and links about Chinese New Year on this site.

INDEX